Our Wild World

ECOSYSTEMS

The EVERGLADES

For Aubrey, remembering the mornings
at Mrazik Pond where it all began
—W. L.

Books for Young Readers
11571 K-Tel Drive
Minnetonka, MN 55343
www.tnkidsbooks.com

Library of Congress Cataloging-in-Publication Data

Lynch, Wayne.
The everglades / text and photographs by Wayne Lynch.
p. cm. -- (Our wild world. Ecosystems)
Includes index.
ISBN 978-1-55971-970-4 (hc) -- ISBN 978-1-55971-971-1 (sc)
1. Natural history--Florida--Everglades. I. Title.

QH105.F6L96 2007

508.759'39--dc22   2006101497

Printed in Singapore
10 9 8 7 6 5 4 3 2 1

The EVERGLADES

Text and Photographs by Wayne Lynch
Assisted by Aubrey Lang

NorthWord
Minnetonka, Minnesota

CONTENTS

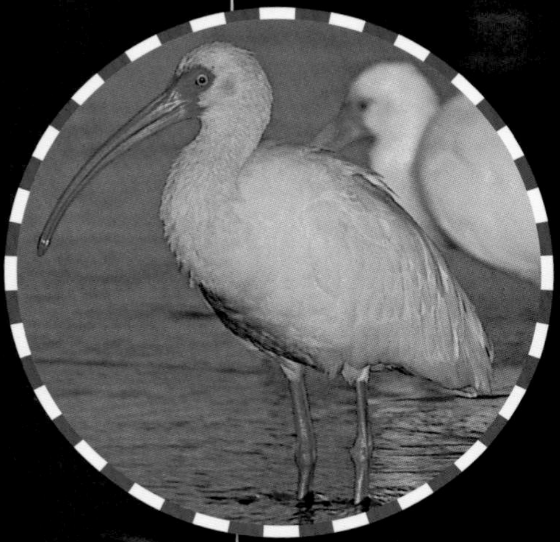

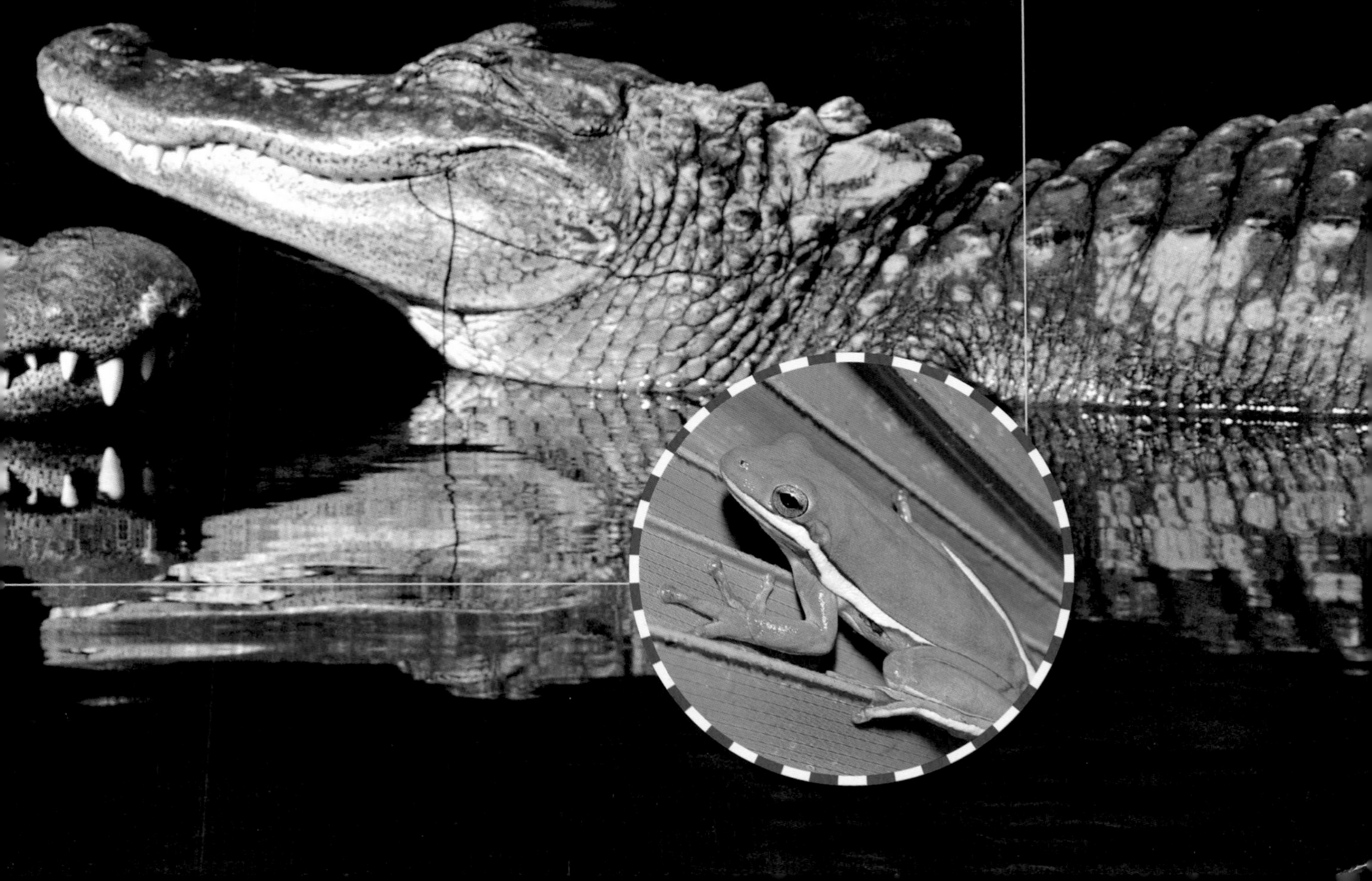

For many years, I thought it would be thrilling to explore a Florida marsh on foot. I wanted to wade through water up to my waist and feel the excitement of being in a wild place where there were alligators and dangerous snakes. Several years ago I made my dream come true. I spent six hours with soggy feet in the flooded sawgrasses of the Florida Everglades. It was an amazing adventure. I vividly recall the white eggs of apple snails stuck to the grasses like clusters of pearls and the pig-like nose of a softshell turtle. I remember turkey vultures circling overhead, and a frightened white-tailed deer as it splashed and leaped away.

One experience was more exciting than all the rest. I was photographing a beautiful flower called an alligator lily when I heard a chirping sound coming from the sawgrass nearby. The sound made me nervous because I didn't recognize it at first. Then, I suddenly remembered that baby alligators make a chirping sound, and I felt really nervous. When I carefully looked around, I saw the mother alligator floating just a few feet (1 m) away from me. Only her dark eyes and the tip of her scaly nose were visible above the water. I soon forgot about the lily and slowly waded away. I was afraid I might splash or trip on an underwater stone, which might make the mother angry and cause her to attack. The mother alligator was much braver than I, and she never moved or even blinked. I will always remember her big shiny eyes watching me as I carefully made my escape.

GRASSY WATERS

TROPICS: warm-weather region near the Earth's equator

THE STATE OF FLORIDA IS LIKE a giant finger pointing south to the warm regions of the tropics. Near the southern tip of the state is the famous freshwater wetland, or marsh, called the Everglades. Before the first European settlers came to Florida, the Everglades was a large river of sawgrass, 40 miles (64 km) wide and 100 miles (161 km) long.

It began on the southern shoreline of Lake Okeechobee, one of the largest lakes in the United States, and stretched south to the warm salty waters of the Gulf of Mexico. Still today, during the summer rainy season, this area floods 1 to 2 feet deep (0.3-0.6 m). But, sawgrass can grow over 9 feet (2.7 m) tall, so most of the plants' leaves and stems are above the water even when it is flooded. The Miccosukee Indians call the Everglades *Pa-hay-okee*, which means "grassy waters."

The Everglades is flat and low. Most of it is only 1 or 2 feet (0.3-0.6 m) above sea level. In Everglades National Park there is a comical sign beside the highway notifying travelers that they are passing a high point in the park—Rock Reef Pass, elevation 3 feet (0.9 m).

Imagine a large flat table, raised on the sides, that slants slightly south toward the Gulf of Mexico. This is the Everglades. The northern

Lake Okeechobee is a very big lake but it is quite shallow. In its deepest part the lake is no deeper than some swimming pools. The word *Okeechobee* comes from the Seminole Indian language and means "big water."

The beautiful clamshell orchid is an endangered species in Florida, although it is common in the Everglades.

boundary of this ecosystem now lies south of Lake Okeechobee. The eastern border is a ridge of limestone covered with pine trees and cabbage palms where gopher tortoises burrow and ghost-like panthers hunt. In the west, the boundary is a thick forest of cypress (SI-pres) trees. Here, there are black bears and otters, snakes and frogs, and more kinds of orchids (OR-kids) than anywhere else in the country. As the river of grass approaches the Gulf of Mexico to the south, it changes to a mangrove forest, the only trees that can grow in the salty ocean water. The Everglades is surrounded by these three different forests.

LIMESTONE: a type of rock made from the skeletons of corals and other ocean creatures

ECO-Fact

More than 40 different kinds of orchids grow in the Everglades. They come in many different shapes and colors such as the white ghost orchid, the purple clamshell orchid, and the yellow dancing lady orchid. Orchids belong to the largest family of flowers on Earth. Worldwide, there are more than 30,000 different kinds. Orchids grow best in hot tropical areas, which is why so many of them grow in the Everglades of southern Florida.

Dry pinelands grow on the east side of the Everglades. In the west there are flooded forests of bald cypress trees, and in the south there are forests of red mangroves. The tangled roots of the mangroves make travel through the forest especially difficult.

PINES AND CABBAGE PALMS

BALD CYPRESSES

RED MANGROVES

ECO-Fact

In the past, Florida was sometimes twice as large as it is today, and at other times it was completely flooded by the ocean. For example, during the Ice Age, when thick ice covered all of Canada and parts of the northern United States, so much of Earth's water was frozen and trapped in the ice that the level of the oceans dropped. This drained the water from large areas of North America, including Florida. Later, when the ice melted, sea levels rose again and large areas of Florida were flooded, including all of the land that is the Everglades today. So, at different times long ago, whales and sharks swam over the Everglades.

Today, half of the Everglades has been drained and destroyed to build houses and huge farms that grow sugarcane and vegetables. Even so, there are still large natural areas of sawgrass filled with wildlife. The Everglades has no towering snow-capped mountains, no fire-spitting volcanoes, no dark ancient forests with giant trees, and no rocky shorelines with crashing waves. Rather, the Everglades is a shy, flat, damp land that at first may seem dull and uninteresting. But when you take a closer look you discover a wild place filled with marvelous secrets. It is these secrets that I want to share with you.

ECO-Fact

A *marsh* is a wetland in which the main plants growing there are sedges, grasses, cattails, and bulrushes, none of which have woody stems. A swamp is different. It is a wetland in which the main plants are trees with woody trunks.

This book is a different kind of nature book than you may have read before. It's a book about an ecosystem, the Everglades ecosystem. *Ecosystem* is the word scientists use to describe all of the plants and animals that live together in a community. It is also about how the richness of the soil, the warmth of the days, and the amount of rainfall affect these animals and plants. In an ecosystem, all these things are connected, and all work together. The Everglades ecosystem is a story about alligators bellowing in the moonlight, and pink-colored spoonbills fishing for food. It is a story about lightning storms and hurricanes, hungry bobcats, and snails as big as golf balls. It is also a story about armor-covered armadillos, rabbits that swim, and turtles that snap.

The bobcat is an excellent hunter. It is fast enough to catch small birds but also strong enough to tackle small deer. Most of the time it eats marsh rabbits, mice, and cotton rats.

The roseate spoonbill is one of the most colorful birds in the Everglades. Adult male and female spoonbills look alike, and both stand almost 3 feet (0.9 m) tall.

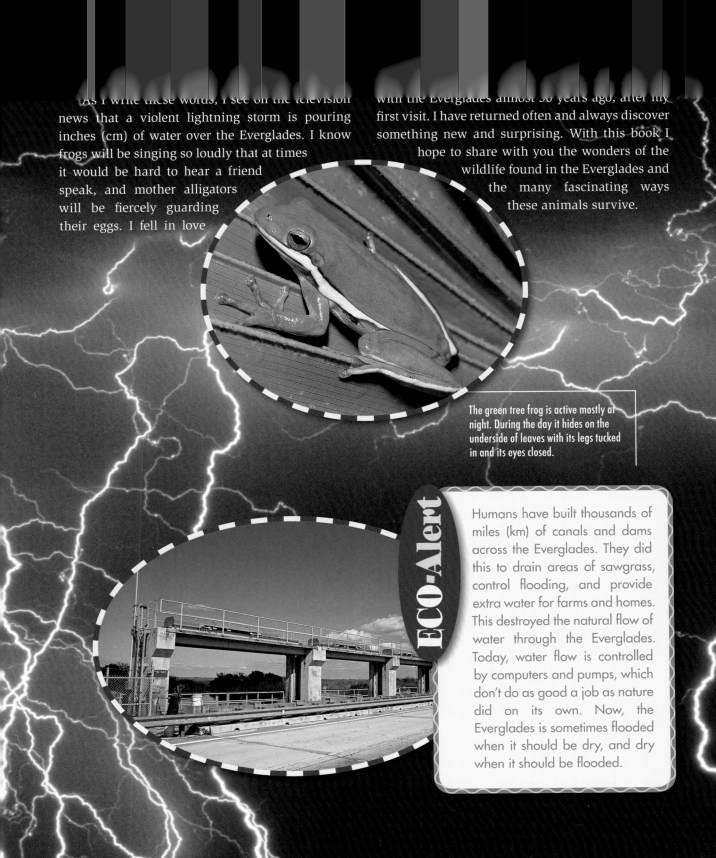

As I write these words, I see on the television news that a violent lightning storm is pouring inches (cm) of water over the Everglades. I know frogs will be singing so loudly that at times it would be hard to hear a friend speak, and mother alligators will be fiercely guarding their eggs. I fell in love with the Everglades almost 30 years ago, after my first visit. I have returned often and always discover something new and surprising. With this book I hope to share with you the wonders of the wildlife found in the Everglades and the many fascinating ways these animals survive.

The green tree frog is active mostly at night. During the day it hides on the underside of leaves with its legs tucked in and its eyes closed.

ECO-Alert

Humans have built thousands of miles (km) of canals and dams across the Everglades. They did this to drain areas of sawgrass, control flooding, and provide extra water for farms and homes. This destroyed the natural flow of water through the Everglades. Today, water flow is controlled by computers and pumps, which don't do as good a job as nature did on its own. Now, the Everglades is sometimes flooded when it should be dry, and dry when it should be flooded.

CHAPTER TWO

One winter, when I was driving through the Everglades, I was surprised to see a large black bear splashing wildly through water up to its shoulders. From the size of the bear's body and the shape of its wide head I guessed that it was probably an adult male bear. In the Everglades, where the winter temperatures are mild, black bears may not hibernate for the winter as their northern cousins do. The bears can stay active because there is enough food for them to eat, such as insects, armadillos, dead deer, wild hogs, berries, and the soft juicy centers of young palm trees.

AIRBOAT: flat-bottomed boat powered by an airplane engine

Moments after I saw the bear, a man on a noisy airboat drove through the sawgrass and raced across the water in a cloud of spray. The man never noticed the bear, and the terrified animal soon disappeared behind a curtain of sawgrass.

RAIN, WIND AND FIRE

NO MATTER WHERE YOU ARE in the Everglades, you are never very far from sawgrass. When the settlers named the plant, they didn't realize it wasn't a grass at all. Sawgrass is actually a sedge. Although sedges look like grasses, they're very different. Sedges grow best in wet areas, which is why they thrive in the Everglades. When the roots of most plants get flooded with water, the plants drown. Not so with sedges. There are many different kinds of sedges in the Everglades, but sawgrass is the most common one, and the one that every visitor sees.

Sawgrass gets its name from the sharp teeth that grow along the edge of its stiff leaves. The leaves are sharp enough to cut a person's skin. Sawgrass grows thickest and tallest in the northern parts of the Everglades where there is more soil. As you move south toward the Gulf of Mexico, the soil gets thinner, and as a result, the sawgrass doesn't grow as high, and the plants grow farther apart. In the north, sawgrass can grow up to 10 feet (3 m) tall, but in the south it is usually less than 4 feet (1.2 m).

Sawgrass grows well in the Everglades for two reasons besides its ability to grow in water. First, it grows well in soil that has very little food in it. And second, it can survive a fire. Fires are common in the Everglades. When flames sweep through the area, the tender growing parts of a sawgrass plant are often underwater and surrounded by a collar of old leaves that protects them from the heat. Fire is actually a friend to sawgrass because it kills any bushes or trees trying to move in. Once the fire passes and the land cools, a sawgrass plant can grow 16 inches (41 cm) in just two weeks!

It's easy to see where the sawgrass got its name when you look closely at the edge of the plant's leaves.

ECO-Alert

Chemicals that farmers use to grow sugarcane and vegetables often drain into the sawgrass marshes of the Everglades. This changes the quality of the water so that cattails and other water plants replace the natural sawgrass. This upsets the ecosystem and causes harm to the animals and plants that live there.

WET SEASON, DRY SEASON

The Everglades' rainy season begins in June and lasts until November. A total of about 60 inches (152 cm) of rain falls on the Everglades every year, and most of the heavy rainstorms occur in summer. Sixty inches is a lot of rain. Compare that to the 40 inches (102 cm) of rain that falls on the forests of Massachusetts, or the 20 inches (51 cm) of rain that soaks the prairies in Colorado. Some of the driest deserts in Arizona get less than 5 inches (13 cm) of rain in a year. In fact, in summer, the Everglades may get more rain in a single day than the deserts get in several years.

Most places in North America have four separate seasons: winter, spring, summer, and autumn. The Everglades, on the other hand, really has only two seasons: a winter dry season, and a summer wet season. The winter dry season runs from about December to May. This is when most people visit, escaping the snowstorms and icy roads of the north. Daytime winter temperatures in the warm and sunny Everglades are between 60°F and 85°F (16-29°C).

Every summer day in the Everglades begins the same. It's always warm and humid. As the morning sun rises, the air heats up even more. Tiny water droplets, too small to see, enter the air from the soggy soil and the many puddles and ponds that cover the land. The summer temperatures in the Everglades are only a few degrees higher than they are on a warm winter day. But, because there is so much moisture in the air during the summer, it feels much warmer. By afternoon, the droplets have clumped together to form fluffy white clouds. Soon the clouds get bigger and turn black and angry-looking. Finally, in the early evening, the stormy sky speaks, and thunder rolls across the sawgrass, soaking it with heavy rain. This is the signal for frogs and toads to sing and mate.

The color of the green anole (an-OH-lee) can quickly change from bright green to gray, tan, or brown. It changes its color when it gets excited or angry. It can also change color with the temperature. In winter, when an anole is cold, it is often dark brown in color. The dark color helps the lizard soak up more heat from the sun.

ECO-Fact

Raccoons have a better sense of touch in their front paws than any other meat-eating animal. They use their sensitive paws to search for crabs, crayfish, clams, frogs, and snails in shallow water. When early settlers saw the animals splashing on the edge of marshes they wrongly thought they were washing their food.

The pig frog, which grunts like a barnyard pig, is the largest frog in the Everglades. It can grow up to 6 inches (15 cm) long.

Every species has its own special croak or peep that sounds different from all other frogs and toads. With practice, a person can learn to recognize each of them. Generally, male frogs and toads call at night when darkness hides them from the sharp eyes of hungry herons, egrets, and red-shouldered hawks. The singing males call as loudly as they can, and as often as possible. They use their voices to show how strong and healthy they are. Female frogs and toads then pick the winners in these singing contests and lay their eggs with them. At the end of the summer rains, the Everglades are crowded with tiny froglets and toadlets.

When I was a boy I learned a fun way to figure out how far away a lightning flash was. This is how you do it. As soon as you see a flash of lightning, start counting slowly: "1 one-thousand, 2 one-thousand, 3 one-thousand," and so on, until you hear the thunder. Once you hear the rumble of the thunder, divide 5 into the number you reached while counting. That will tell you how many miles away the lighting flash was. For example, if you are able to count to "10 one-thousand" between seeing the flash and hearing the thunder, you divide 10 by 5 and you know that the lightning is roughly 2 miles (3.2 km) away.

Thunderstorms boom across the Everglades 90 days of the year, which is more often than anywhere else in the United States. Where there is thunder, there must always be lightning. Inside the large black storm clouds of summer, electricity builds up. Eventually, when the electricity gets strong enough, it travels through the air like a giant spark. During a lightning flash, the air along the path of the spark gets heated to a temperature that is five times hotter than the surface of the sun. This heated air swells so fast that it produces the loud boom that we call thunder.

Most lightning flashes never leave the sky. They stay inside the black towering clouds where they are born. But when lightning does strike the ground it can set the land on fire. A bolt of lightning can make an Everglades palm tree explode into flame as if a bomb went off. If the flames spread to the sawgrass nearby, great areas of the Everglades can go up in smoke. The dry tops of the sawgrass burn quickly, but their roots stay wet in the moist soil, and allow the plant to grow again.

Every summer, lightning starts a dozen or more fires in the Everglades. If the fires are small, as most of them are, wildlife can usually escape the flames. But when large areas burn, some animals may die. The victims are then eaten by vultures, or their ashes mix with the soil and make it richer for the next crop of sawgrass. Lightning, fire, death, and re-growth have always been a natural part of the Everglades.

Turkey vultures have good vision. But they also have a good sense of smell and they use this to find dead animals killed by fires in the Everglades.

Hurricanes are the most powerful and dangerous summer storms in the Everglades. Every year, three or four of them batter different parts of Florida, and they often sweep across the Everglades. All hurricanes start life in one of three areas: in the tropical waters off the west coast of Africa; in the Gulf of Mexico; or in the Caribbean Sea. In all three areas, the sun is hot, and by July the saltwater heats up. As the water warms, it produces storm clouds that spin and slowly move across the ocean like a giant funnel. Sometimes these spinning tropical storms slow down and disappear, but at other times they speed up and grow larger. When the winds inside a tropical storm reach 75 miles (120 km) per hour, scientists call the storm a hurricane.

More than half of all hurricanes occur in September and October. Scientists believe there will be more hurricanes in the future, and they may be stronger than they are today. The reason for this is that the temperature of the atmosphere surrounding the Earth is slowly rising. This problem is called global warming. It is happening because humans all over the world are burning too much coal, gasoline, and natural gas in their vehicles, homes, and factories. When these fuels are burned, harmful smoke and gases escape into the atmosphere and the climate of the planet gets warmer.

CLIMATE: the different types of weather that occur in an area

Some large hurricanes can be over 600 miles (1000 km) wide from edge to edge. The center of a hurricane is called the eye.

Damage from a hurricane is caused by wind, storm surge, and rain. Winds in a hurricane can blow at 180 miles (290 km) per hour, which is strong enough to snap a tree trunk in half and blow a house away. The sawgrasses of the Everglades simply bend flat, even in the strongest winds, and they are usually not damaged. Most birds and animals survive the winds by sheltering close to the ground.

In the past, birds, spiders, and butterflies from Cuba and other Caribbean countries were sometimes captured by hurricanes and blown many miles (km) across the ocean to Florida. Today, many tropical animals including black-and-yellow zebra butterflies and white-crowned pigeons live year-round in the Everglades.

Storm surges are the high tides that come with hurricanes. At times, the water can rise up to 15 feet (4.6 m) above normal and flood the lands that are close to the ocean. In a hurricane, if too much saltwater floods into the freshwater sawgrass marshes of the Everglades, the plants may die from the saltiness.

Heavy rains can also cause damage in a hurricane. An average hurricane may dump 6 to 8 inches (15-20 cm) of rain in a single day. The heaviest rainfall in Florida history occurred during a hurricane in 1941 when 35 inches (89 cm) of rain fell in just two days. Heavy rainfall can sometimes kill nesting birds in the Everglades by flooding their eggs, chilling their chicks, or drowning them. Downpours can also flood animals out of their burrows. Most of the time, however, all of the birds and animals survive.

TIDES: the rise and fall of the ocean twice each day

In past centuries, the strong winds in hurricanes sometimes carried insects such as this zebra butterfly and birds such as these Caribbean flamingos from the tropics to the Everglades.

The male magnificent frigatebird inflates a scarlet throat pouch to attract a mate. Frigatebirds normally live in the Florida Keys, but these skilled soaring seabirds are sometimes carried into the Everglades by storms.

The wildlife of the Everglades is the part of the ecosystem that I love the best. There are three important wildlife habitats in the Everglades: shallow sawgrass marshes; gator holes and sloughs (SLEWS) where the water is deep; and forest-covered tree islands. In the following chapters I will introduce you to some of the interesting creatures that live in each of these three wildlife habitats. Some Everglades animals live their entire lives in only one of these habitats, such as the barred owl that lives only on tree islands. Others, like the Virginia opossum (a-PAW-sum), wander across all three habitats. So, when I talk about an animal in a certain habitat that doesn't mean it can't live anywhere else in the Everglades.

HABITAT:
the natural home
where an
animal lives

23

"I love vultures—partly because everyone thinks they are such ugly birds and I have always had a soft spot in my heart for unpopular creatures. Besides that, vultures are very interesting birds. The Everglades is a great place to watch turkey vultures and black vultures. At night, they gather in large groups to sleep in specially chosen trees. One morning, I got up before sunrise to photograph the birds waking up. A dense fog hung close to the ground, which made the world appear gray and gloomy. The vultures were spaced out in the tops of a few trees, surrounded by sawgrass as far as I could see. Some of the birds were perched so closely together they almost touched each other. As the golden light of sunrise struck the treetops, dozens of vultures suddenly opened their great black wings at the same time. They looked as if they were praying to the sun. Actually, they were just trying to warm up after a cool night.

Many minutes passed, and suddenly, as if they received a secret signal, they all flew off. After a few flaps, each bird spread its wings wide open to let the hot air rising from the ground lift it into the sky. Soon, there were several hundred vultures circling together, rising higher and higher. After soaring as high as they could go, they glided away in different directions, searching for animals that had died during the night."

SHALLOW SAWGRASS MARSHES

SAWGRASS MARSHES COVER roughly three-quarters of the Everglades. The water level in the sawgrass varies throughout the year because of the wet season and dry season. During the summer wet season the water may be 2 feet (0.6 m) deep. In the winter dry season, there may be only a few inches (cm) of water, or none at all.

These three male pintail ducks are searching for seeds underwater. Dozens of different kinds of ducks spend winter in the Everglades.

Small mosquito fish, crayfish, snails, and frogs live in the shallow water of the sawgrass marshes. These animals, in turn, attract hungry predators such as herons, egrets, ibises, water snakes, and raccoons. Ducks also come to the marshes to feed on sawgrass seeds and on the many other water plants that grow

PREDATOR: an animal that hunts and kills other animals for food

there. When the marshes dry out, opossums and vultures search for dead animals that got stranded when the water disappeared. Some of the fish and frogs burrow into the mud and wait for rain. Apple snails also bury themselves in the mud and cover their body with sticky slime to keep from drying out.

ECO-Fact

An apple snail is the size of a golf ball. Being so big makes them a good source of food for many creatures, including alligators, river otters, raccoons, and birds such as limpkins and grackles. One bird, the snail kite, eats nothing but apple snails. The kite has a long hooked beak that it uses to pull the snail out of its shell.

ECO-Alert

A "swamp buggy" is a special kind of truck used to travel through the Everglades. It has huge tires that can drive through deep water and muddy sawgrass marshes without getting stuck. Swamp buggies, like airboats, are noisy and scare wildlife. They also crush and kill plants and can cause permanent ruts in the mud.

NATURE'S BALDIES •••

Most people recognize vultures as large black birds with no feathers on their head. The bare skin on a turkey vulture's head is red. The skin on a black vulture is black. There are several good reasons why vultures have no feathers on their head and face. If a vulture gets overheated after sitting in the hot sun too long it can simply increase the blood going to its face, where there are no feathers to hold in the heat. This decreases body temperature and cools down the bird.

A vulture can also use the colors in its face to quickly tell other vultures what kind of mood it is in. For example, the facial colors in a hungry, excited turkey vulture are usually much brighter than they are in a bird that is calm. The same thing happens when people get angry and their face turns red.

Probably the most important benefit of a naked head is that it keeps the vulture clean. When a vulture feeds on a dead animal, its head can get dirty and smeared with dried blood and rotting bits of flesh. With bare skin on its head, it is easier for the vulture to clean itself afterward than if its head were covered with feathers.

The vultures in the Everglades have a second way to cool themselves if they get too hot. They can poop on their legs. Bird poop contains water. By squirting it on their legs, vultures can cool themselves off. A vulture that is overheated may poop on one leg and then the other every few minutes, until it finally cools down. When the birds do this, the skin on their legs get painted white from the poop.

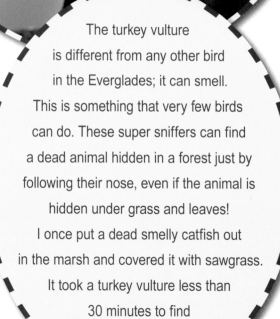

The turkey vulture is different from any other bird in the Everglades; it can smell. This is something that very few birds can do. These super sniffers can find a dead animal hidden in a forest just by following their nose, even if the animal is hidden under grass and leaves! I once put a dead smelly catfish out in the marsh and covered it with sawgrass. It took a turkey vulture less than 30 minutes to find the rotting fish.

LONG-LEGGED  BEAUTIES

No one can travel through the Everglades without seeing elegant long-legged birds wading in the shallow water next to the roads. These wading birds are the glamorous movie stars of the Everglades. My favorites are the great egret with lacy white plumes on its back, the white ibis with its graceful curved red bill and bright blue eyes, and the roseate (ro-zee-ATE) spoonbill with feathers as pink as a sunset.

Thirteen species of wading birds hunt in the shallow waters of the sawgrass. In nature, when birds live together, they sometimes compete with each other for food. This is the case with the wading birds in the Everglades. To lessen competition with each other, they go about things differently: they are active at different times of the day; they hunt in different depths of water; and they use slightly different areas of the marsh. Their diets also vary, and they have different ways of capturing their food.

The roseate spoonbill, like all wading birds, spends many hours every day scratching and cleaning its feathers to keep them waterproof.

White ibises

This yellow-crowned night-heron was hunting for fiddler crabs along the edge of the water in broad daylight. Normally they hunt at night.

A black-crowned night-heron

Most wading birds hunt during the day. In the Everglades, the two exceptions are the yellow-crowned and black-crowned night-herons. Both have large eyes to help them see better at night when they hunt for fish, crabs, and crayfish. The black-crowned night-heron even hunts the newly-hatched chicks of other wading birds, attacking the chicks at night when the herons can sneak close to their nests.

The wood stork is an endangered species. Like the ibises and spoonbill, this big bird also uses touch to catch its food. The stork hunts with its beak dipped in the water. It wades along like this and slowly stirs the water with one of its feet. When a frightened fish touches the edge of its beak, the stork snaps it up faster than you can snap your fingers. Because the stork is using touch and not its eyes to capture food, it can hunt in muddy water and in water that is filled with weeds.

This is a young wood stork. The head of an adult bird has no feathers and is covered with gray warty skin. Because of this, the wood stork's nickname is "flinthead."

ENDANGERED: a species that is in danger of disappearing from the wild

The wading birds with the longest legs, such as the great blue heron and the great egret, hunt in the deepest water. These birds have two ways of catching their food. They stand perfectly still in the water and wait for a fish to swim by, or they wade very slowly, watching for movement in the water. The white ibis and snowy egret have shorter legs and they hunt closer to shore. The snowy egret also has bright yellow feet that it uses underwater to frighten fish and drive them closer to the surface where it can catch them. The small herons such as the little blue heron and green-backed heron hunt at the edge of the water where they search the shallows for fish, crayfish, tadpoles, frogs, and insects.

ECO-Fact

Most grasshoppers are brown or green in color to help them hide from hungry birds. The lubber grasshopper is bright orange. The bright color is meant to advertise that the insect is dangerous to eat. This large hopper—3 inches (7.6 cm) long—has sharp spines on its rear legs and a powerful kick to defend itself. It can also squirt out a bitter fluid from its stomach and a poisonous foam from under its wings.

Each of these waders has a unique way of catching its meal. Herons and egrets have good eyesight and long sharp bills that they use to stab their food or to grab it. The white ibis and glossy ibis use their long curved bills to poke and search underwater, mostly for things they cannot see. Generally, they find their food by touch, using their sensitive beaks like fingertips. The roseate spoonbill is another wading bird that uses touch to catch its food. The spoonbill has a broad, flattened beak with a spoon-shaped tip. It sweeps its open bill back and forth in the water scooping up tiny fish, crabs, beetles, and shrimp.

Little blue herons most often hunt alone, although they sometimes feed in groups when food is especially plentiful.

OPOSSUMS IN A POUCH

One of the first American settlers to describe the Virginia opossum said it was the size of a housecat, had a tail like a rat, and a head like a pig. Most amazing of all, it had a pouch on its belly where it nursed and carried its young. The opossum not only looks strange, but it raises its babies differently than any other mammal in the United States.

Baby opossums are born after growing inside their mother for only 12 days. Compare that with a puppy that is born after about 63 days, and a human baby that is born after 280 days. Because baby opossums are born so soon, they are very small. Twenty of them can fit in the hollow of a teaspoon!

Newborn opossums are blind and naked. The tiny pink babies crawl through the fur on their mother's belly, and once they find the opening to her pouch, they tumble in. As many as a dozen babies may squeeze inside at one time, though the average litter size is eight. Inside the pouch, each attaches to a nipple and begins to nurse. They don't

To "play 'possum" is a slang expression that describes a person pretending to be dead. Opossums sometimes do this when a dangerous predator, such as a dog, threatens them. When pretending to be dead, an opossum lies perfectly still on its side and drools foamy spit from its mouth. Sometimes it also poops at the same time. Scientists think that this unusual behavior may confuse a predator so that it leaves the opossum unharmed.

leave the pouch for almost two months. When the babies grow too large to fit inside the pouch, they ride on their mother's back.

Opossums will eat almost anything. This explains why they can live in every type of habitat in the Everglades. Their usual diet includes berries, fruits, earthworms, grasshoppers, crickets, bird eggs, frogs, lizards, and snakes. Like vultures, they also eat dead animals. The opossum's sharp sense of smell helps it find food at night when it does most of its hunting.

ECO-Fact

The marsh rabbit is a funny bunny that lives in the wet areas of the Everglades. It doesn't hop like other rabbits, but walks or runs instead. It even swims, and will run to the water when it is scared. In the warm Everglades, a mother marsh rabbit may raise six families of young in a single year and give birth to a total of 18 babies!

CHAPTER FOUR

One afternoon in the Everglades I decided to watch which animals would come to a small water hole that was slowly drying up. Soon an alligator dragged itself onto the mud to warm up in the sun, and an egret flew in to hunt along the water's edge. Then, out of the corner of my eye, I saw a snake. It was rusty brown with dark brown blotches on its back. When I saw the yellow tip on its tail I knew it was a cottonmouth, a dangerous venomous (VEN-uh-mus) snake. The crafty snake wiggles the tip of its tail like a worm to lure hungry lizards and frogs into coming closer for a snack, and then they get eaten themselves. I was curious to see what the snake would catch for lunch today.

VENOMOUS:
poison-producing

The cottonmouth coiled itself among some water plants lying on the mud and I moved in closer for a better look. The snake was swallowing a small fish that had died when the water hole began to dry up. I quickly grabbed my camera and had just enough time to capture the action on film. The fish was gone in a matter of minutes, and the satisfied snake quietly slithered away.

DEEP SLOUGHS AND GATOR HOLES

EVEN THOUGH THE EVERGLADES is a wetland, parts of it may dry out. This usually happens during the winter season when there is much less rain than in summer. Luckily, the Everglades has areas of deeper water, called sloughs, that never dry up.

A friend of mine who studies insects calls the beautiful damselfly "a toothpick with wings." Damselflies use their large eyes to hunt and track small flies and mosquitoes.

These sloughs are scattered throughout the sawgrass marshes. Fish and frogs escape to the deeper water in sloughs as soon as the sawgrass begins to dry up. Sloughs can also attract hundreds of wading birds. It's quite a show when egrets, herons, storks, spoonbills, and ibises crowd together in a single slough, each hunting in its own special way.

Not all of the wildlife in the Everglades can reach a slough when the sawgrass marshes begin to dry up. Alligators solve the problem. Thousands of alligators live in the Everglades, and many don't live near sloughs where they can find deep water in the winter dry season. So, they dig their own deep water refuges, called gator holes.

The white spider lily grows in deep water and has a pleasant smell.

Alligators use their claws and jaws to dig holes in the mud and then they pile the mud around the edges. They tear up the sawgrass and other water plants to clear a pool of open water in the center of the hole. The open-water pool is usually 2 to 4 feet (0.6-1.2 m) deeper than the surrounding marsh and as large as 20 feet (6 m) across. Over time, willows and other bushes grow on the soil piled around the edges of the gator hole. Large gator holes may hold over 100 alligators. They may be used for many years by many different alligators, becoming a permanent part of the Everglades ecosystem.

Gator holes are a vital part of the Everglades. Like sloughs, they provide important deep-water homes for insects, fish, turtles, frogs, crayfish, and crabs during the winter dry season. In turn, these small animals attract wading birds, otters, mink, raccoons, snakes, hawks, and vultures.

Without gator holes, a great many animals and birds in the Everglades would not survive the winter dry season. Once the summer rains return, the sawgrass marshes flood again. The wildlife can then escape from the crowded conditions of the gator hole and spread across the Everglades once more.

Adult male alligators start to bellow in late winter. The bellow of an alligator serves the same purpose as the bugle of a bull elk or the roar of a male lion. It is a way for males to tell females that they are looking for a partner. It also frightens other males away. Females want to mate with the strongest, healthiest bull alligator around so that their babies will grow up to be healthy like their father.

It is the mother alligator's job to build a nest for her babies. She tears up sawgrass, cattails, willows, and other water plants and builds a mound about 3 feet (0.9 m) high and 5 feet (1.5 m) across. This is where she will lay her 30 eggs. By the time she lays her eggs in June, the summer rains have started. The wet sawgrass in her nest rots in the sunshine, creating heat and keeping the eggs warm. During this time, the mother guards the nest from raccoons and other predators. The eggs hatch in late August, during the peak of the hurricane season, but most of the babies survive these summer storms and move to a nearby gator hole. A newborn baby alligator is only 9 inches (23 cm) long and an easy meal for herons and egrets, so the mother continues to guard and protect them.

From the moment a young alligator hatches, it must find its own food. Crayfish, snails, and insects are its first meals. As it gets larger, the alligator switches to fish, turtles, birds, and small mammals, such as rice rats and muskrats. A young alligator will stay in its mother's gator hole until it is roughly three years old and about 3 feet (0.9 m) long. After that, it leaves and searches for a new place to live in the sawgrass marsh. Not many predators will attack a 3-foot alligator except

other alligators. I once saw a dead 3-foot alligator floating on its back in a gator hole. An 8-foot (2.4-m) alligator was floating nearby guarding it. Alligators will eat their own kind and that's likely what the larger alligator was planning to do.

When a young female alligator is about five years old she can start raising a family of her own. Young male alligators must wait a few more years to become fathers because they have to grow large enough to win fights with other males.

These baby alligators which were only about 12 inches (30 cm) long were soaking up the warm sunshine on a cool winter day.

One time when I was exploring the edge of a sawgrass marsh a mother alligator roared and rushed at me with her mouth wide open. I jumped so high that I'm sure the birds thought I could fly. I had accidentally come too close to some baby alligators and the mother just wanted to frighten me away. She did. Alligators are magnificent reptiles that have been on Earth since the dinosaurs ruled, more than 100 million years ago. If you want to discover how dinosaurs may have lived long ago, you can watch an alligator today.

WATER-LOVING
WEASELS

Two members of the weasel family, the river otter and the mink, live in the watery world of the Everglades. The mink, which is rare, hunts in shallow water where it searches for small mammals, birds, frogs, crayfish, crabs, fish, and snakes. It generally avoids deep water where alligators and snapping turtles might attack and eat it. The mink must also watch out for many other enemies including cottonmouths, indigo snakes, bobcats, hawks, and great horned owls. The Everglades mink is the smallest mink in North America. Adult females weigh as little as 1 pound (0.5 kg). That's less than a gray squirrel. No wonder so many hungry predators hunt them for lunch—they're practically bite-size for many animals.

ECO-Alert

Some of the wildlife in the Everglades is colorful and beautiful, while others are cute and easily tamed. As a result, people collect them illegally from the wild to keep as pets or to display in boxes. This has caused many of these animals to become rare, such as multi-colored tree snails, golden Everglades rat snakes, indigo snakes, gopher tortoises, and box turtles.

Although mink are strong swimmers, they are not very good hunters underwater. They can only hold their breath for 20 or 30 seconds, and their eyesight underwater is blurry, like it is for humans, so they can't see very well.

The river otter, unlike the mink, is an underwater expert. It can hold its breath for up to four minutes in a dive and its thick waterproof fur coat keeps it from getting cold. In the water, the otter is an acrobat.

It can swim and swerve quickly because it has webbed feet like a duck and a strong flat tail that helps it to steer.

The river otter hunts in deeper water than the mink. As a result, you can see otters more often in sloughs and large gator holes than in sawgrass marshes. The otter is a fish lover, and in the Everglades it hunts catfish, sunfish, and gar.

Male river otters stay with their mate for just a few days in the spring. The mother raises the babies by herself.

WHIRLIGIGS AND WATER STRIDERS

Insects are the most common animals in the Everglades, yet visitors often overlook them because they are small. Two of my favorite insects, the water strider and the whirligig beetle, occur everywhere in the Everglades. Both of them live on the surface of the water and use ripples to hunt and talk to each other.

The whirligig beetle is a round, black beetle that spins and speeds across the surface of the water. Its eyes are split in half. One half of each eye looks underwater while the other half looks above the water. Even more important than its eyesight is its sense of touch. The whirligig's two antennae (an-TEN-ee) touch the surface of the water so that it can feel the ripples that bounce off objects in its path. This is how the whirligig keeps from crashing into things. The beetles can swerve very fast. I have watched dozens of whirligigs swim around in the same patch of water without crashing into each other. Whirligig beetles are like miniature bumper cars that never bump together. The whirligig is a predator and it also uses ripples to find dying insects splashing on the surface.

ECO-Fact

Scientists have found at least 43 different species of blood-sucking mosquitoes in the Everglades. In the rainy summer months the mosquitoes can be so thick that they continually fly into your nose and mouth and make travel in the Everglades very uncomfortable.

Whirligigs sometimes clump together like this as a way to protect themselves from predators.

The water strider spreads its weight out over its four long legs. In this way it doesn't fall through the surface and it can skate along as if it were on ice.

The water strider also lives on the top of the water. It skates along the surface and rows with its middle pair of long legs. The water strider, like the whirligig, also uses ripples to find its food. When an insect from below comes to the surface for air, the water strider feels the ripples and stabs the insect with its sharp mouth. It quickly pumps chemicals into the victim like a spider does. The chemicals turn the insides of the prey animal into soup and the water strider slurps it up like a milkshake. The empty shell of the prey drifts to the bottom.

PREY: an animal that is killed by another animal for food

Water striders also use ripples to talk to each other. When a male strider wants to charm a female, he taps on the water and sends out a love letter of ripples across the surface. If a female comes close, the male taps the water faster to create more ripples to win her heart. Each species of water strider uses a different pattern of ripples to communicate.

A TOUGH TURTLE: THE SNAPPER

Nine kinds of freshwater turtles live in the Everglades. Most of them can pull their head inside their bony shell to protect themselves when a dangerous predator attacks. The snapping turtle can't do this because its shell is too small. So, to defend itself, it snaps and bites with lightning speed.

The snapping turtle is a large, powerful turtle that can weigh over 40 pounds (18 kg). With a single bite, it can cut off a child's finger. Only a large alligator or a black bear would dare to attack an adult snapping turtle.

Scientists are not certain why the front claws on a snapping turtle are so long and heavy since they are not used for digging or in defending itself.

The snapping turtle probably spends more time in the water than any other turtle in the Everglades. Unlike other turtles, this one rarely climbs onto logs or stones to warm itself in the sunshine. Instead, it floats at the surface of the water, or buries itself in the mud underwater with only its eyes and nose uncovered.

The "snapper" hunts at night. It crawls along the muddy bottom underwater and searches for dead animals, crabs, frogs, salamanders, and fish. It also eats baby ducks, gulls, and coots. When a snapping turtle catches a large bird such as a coot it usually drags it underwater and holds it there until it drowns. The turtles also eat many different types of water plants. One scientist joked that a snapping turtle will eat anything it can fit inside its mouth.

Like all turtles, the snapping turtle must come on to dry land to dig a nest and lay its eggs. A big female turtle may lay as many as 21 eggs. The eggs normally hatch at the end of summer, but the baby turtles may stay buried underground until the following spring. Nearly half of all snapping turtle nests are destroyed by raccoons and skunks that eat the eggs.

ECO-Fact

The anhinga (ann-HING-gah) is also called the "snakebird" because of the way it swims through the water with only its head and neck exposed, resembling a swimming snake. An anhinga's feathers get completely soaked when it swims, so afterward it must dry off in the sun with its wings stretched out.

CHAPTER FIVE

Many animals in the Everglades are only active at night. To see them, I drive slowly along back roads and use a spotlight. This is a good way to see opossums, raccoons, and bobcats, which often travel along the edges of the roads. One night I even saw a Florida panther run across the road. There are only a few panthers living in the Everglades and seeing one is a thrill.

Snakes are the animals I see most often during a night drive. The pavement on the highway heats up after a hot day and it stays warm for many hours after the sun goes down. Snakes stretch out on the warm roads at night to soak up some of the heat. I have found many water snakes doing this, as well as cottonmouths, rat snakes, and king snakes.

On a recent night drive, I almost hit a large tree branch that was lying across the road. As I passed, I realized it wasn't a branch at all. It was a huge Burmese python. I stopped the car and ran back just as the snake was disappearing into the bushes. A Burmese python can grow up to 20 feet (6 m) long and weigh over 200 pounds (91 kg). These snakes come from India and Southeast Asia, but now many of them live wild in the Everglades. Most of them were released by careless pet owners who couldn't handle them any longer after the snakes grew too large to keep at home.

TREE ISLANDS

ALTHOUGH THE EVERGLADES IS MAINLY a sawgrass wetland, islands of trees are scattered throughout this wetland. These tree islands can be smaller than a football field, or many times larger. Some tree islands are covered with willow bushes and others are covered with tall cypress trees. These islands sometimes get flooded for brief periods during the summer rains but they dry out in the winter.

A tropical hammock is one type of tree island that rarely gets flooded because it is high above the water level. This creates a nice, dry home for many kinds of plants and trees to grow—a greater variety than on any other kind of tree island. The word *hammock* comes from the Seminole Indian language and means house or home. In earlier times, when the Seminoles lived in the Everglades, they often built their villages on these dry lush tree islands.

Hammocks are called tropical because most of the trees that grow there are found nowhere else in the United States and they are usually found only in tropical areas farther south. This isn't as surprising as it sounds. If you carefully examine a map of the United States, you can see that the center of the Everglades is actually closer to the tropical islands of Cuba and the Bahamas than it is to Florida's northern border with Georgia. Seeds from tropical plants and trees have been carried by the wind or ocean currents from Cuba and the Bahamas to the Everglades. Over thousands of years, this happened many times.

Tree islands, especially the tropical hammocks, are shady sanctuaries (SANK-choo-air-eez) where animals can stay cool, hide, and find food. The leafy trees in hammocks provide shade and keep the air cooler than in the surrounding marshes. Many of the vines and bushes on tree islands produce berries that are good to eat. For example, the cabbage palm has juicy black fruits the size of peas. These fruits are eaten by black bears, raccoons, cardinals, robins, blue jays, and fish crows. Tree islands provide protection because the ground is often thick with roots and holes where wildlife can hide from danger. Songbirds and small mammals shelter in such cracks to escape the strong winds of hurricanes.

Blue jays and black bears are attracted to tree islands for hiding places, for shelter from bad weather, and for food.

Many people have let animals that do not belong in the Everglades go free there. Other people have planted trees that also do not belong there. These foreign plants and animals create serious problems for the Everglades, such as choking out native species and disrupting food chains. Some of the worst invaders are Brazilian pepper trees from South America, paperbark trees from Australia, walking catfish from Asia, and blue tilapia fish from Africa.

The juicy red berries of the Brazilian pepper are eaten by many birds in the Everglades.

A great egret perched in the setting sun moments before it flew to a safe roost for the night.

ECO-Fact

Thornbugs are a type of insect that suck the sap out of plants. The thorn on their back makes them difficult to swallow and this protects them from hungry birds.

You can certainly see how the strangler fig got its name. It looks almost as if some alien has attached itself to the tree's mighty trunk.

Some of the tropical trees that grow in hammocks have interesting names, such as poisonwood, cabbage palm, strangler fig, and gumbo limbo. I think it's fun to learn how plants got their names. For example, the sap of poisonwood causes an itchy rash if it gets on your skin. The lower part of a cabbage palm's leaves were eaten as a vegetable by the Indians. The strangler fig actually kills other trees. It slowly grows around them and eventually shades them to death. The gumbo limbo is also called the tourist tree by people in the West Indies. That's because the tree has red peeling bark, like the skin of tourists when they stay in the sun too long.

The red peeling bark of the gumbo limbo is how the tree keeps other plants from growing on its trunk and branches.

SUN-SEEKING AIR PLANTS

One of the first things you notice when you walk through a tropical hammock is that the branches and trunks of the trees have other plants growing on them. These plants are called air plants. Plants that grow on the ground use their roots to soak up water and food from the soil. Air plants use their roots to anchor themselves to the rough bark of trees, but their roots don't steal any food from the trees. Air plants get their water from rainwater that dribbles down the bark or falls on their leaves. Their food comes from dust and bits of dead plants that get trapped around their roots. An air plant wants only one thing from the tree on which it grows. It wants to be high off the ground where it can capture as much sunlight as possible.

In the Everglades, there are many kinds of air plants, including big leafy ferns, yellow and pink orchids, and spiky bromeliads (bro-MEE-lee-ads). There is even one kind of cactus that grows as an air plant. This may be surprising because cactuses usually grow in dry deserts. But life high in these tree islands can also be dry.

Bromeliads are the most common air plants in the Everglades. Many look like wild pineapple plants with spiky tops. Most of them trap rainwater in a bowl of leaves in the center of the plant. The biggest bromeliads can hold enough water to fill four empty cans of soda pop. Many small animals live in the tiny pools inside bromeliads. Since there are no fish in these pools, it is a safe place for insects and frogs to hide and lay their eggs. The bromeliads benefit as well. These small animals poop in the pools and their poop becomes valuable food for the bromeliads.

One hungry bromeliad has a deadly secret—it's an insect hunter. The inside leaves of the plant are covered with a slippery powder. When an insect flies in for a visit, the powder causes it to slide into the pool of water and drown. The dead insect soon turns to liquid, and the plant soaks up the nutritious (new-TRISH-us) soup.

Inside this large bromeliad I found a small puddle of water with a green tree frog living there.

ECO-Fact

Tree snails come in many different colors with stripes that are yellow, brown, green, or pink. To me, they look like Christmas tree ornaments. During the day the snails stick to the smooth bark of trees. At night, they move around to find food. They use their tongue like a sharp file to scrape off tiny plants to eat. Often, each tree island has its own variety of colorful tree snail that is found nowhere else.

THE AMAZING ARMADILLO

No animal can be confused with the armadillo (ARM-a-dillo). The name *armadillo* comes from the Spanish language and means "little armored one." I once held one of these animals in my hands. The thick shell on its back was not hard like the shell of a turtle. It felt like thick rubber. Even its tail was protected by thick rubbery scales. It had small black eyes, bare pink ears, and a wet nose that wiggled around a lot.

In the Everglades, the most likely place to see an armadillo is on a dry tree island. Here it uses its nose like a shovel to dig in the dirt for insects and grubs. But the armadillo is also completely at home in wet areas. Surprisingly, it is a good swimmer, even though it looks as though it would sink like a rock. Before it goes for a swim, an armadillo swallows some air to fill its stomach. This helps it to float. Then, it paddles over the surface of the water like a dog. If it wants to cross quickly to another island it can simply hold its breath and walk along the bottom.

Many armadillos have scars on their back. Others are missing the end of their tail or parts of their ears. Bobcats, black bears, and alligators are common predators of the armadillo and likely cause many of these injuries. However, the biggest killer of the armadillo is the automobile. When a vehicle passes over an armadillo that is crossing the highway, the animal's first reaction is to leap straight into the air. This escape plan might work against a bobcat, but it means certain death with an automobile. Even its tough, rubbery armor can't protect it from that.

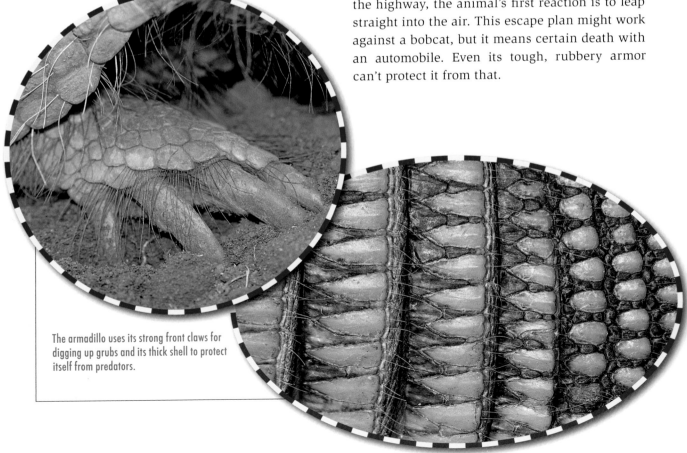

The armadillo uses its strong front claws for digging up grubs and its thick shell to protect itself from predators.

The armadillo is a recent settler in Florida. In 1924, some armadillos escaped from a zoo during a hurricane. A couple of years later, a few more got free when a circus truck turned over and crashed. It wasn't long before armadillos multiplied and lived everywhere in Florida, including the Everglades.

SPIDER SILK

My wife, Aubrey, likes spiders, and because of her, I got interested in them too. Tree islands in the Everglades are a good place to look for crab spiders, wolf spiders, jumping spiders, and funnel-web spiders. The biggest spider of them all is the golden orb spider. The female's body can be almost an inch (2.5 cm) long and its legs can reach from one side of your hand to the other. Golden orb spiders can build webs larger than a kitchen table, where they catch big prey such as dragonflies with their sticky threads. Some experts say that the golden orb spider produces the strongest silk of any spider.

The wolf spider pictured above has eight eyes. The two large eyes in the front are what the spider uses to hunt for food. The large female golden orb spider pictured below was sitting in the center of her web which was more than 3 feet (0.9 m) across.

Everyone knows that spiders spin webs of silk and use these to trap their food. But, did you know that spiders use silk in other ways as well? Every spider has special tubes on the rear tip of its body. Each tube produces a different type of silk. One type of silk acts as a safety line, also called a dragline. Wherever a spider goes, it drags a safety line behind it. If a spider accidentally falls or jumps to escape danger, it can climb back up the safety line. A spider's dragline is just like the safety rope that a mountain climber uses.

Female spiders use a special silk to wrap around their eggs to make an egg sac. Some mother spiders attach the egg sac to the edge of their web where they can guard it. Mother black widow spiders move the egg sac around during the day so that the sunshine keeps the eggs warm. Mother wolf spiders don't spin a web. They attach their egg sac to the rear tip of their body and carry it around like a backpack wherever they go.

When baby spiders finally hatch, they have an easy and fast way to leave their mother. First they climb to the top of a bush or a tall stalk of sawgrass. Then they produce a long thread of silk. The wind catches the thread and carries them away like a kite. This behavior is called ballooning. It can carry a baby spider many miles (km) away from its mother to a new home. You can imagine how far they might be carried during a hurricane. Such strong winds could easily carry a spider from Cuba to the Everglades, which is how some of them got there in the first place.

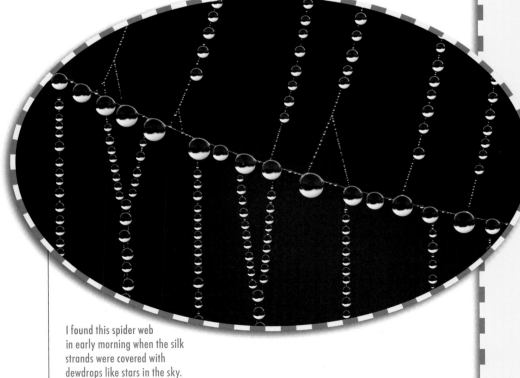

I found this spider web in early morning when the silk strands were covered with dewdrops like stars in the sky.

SCIENTISTS SAVE THE PANTHER

The Florida panther is the same animal as the mountain lion, cougar, and puma of the western mountains of North America. A few years ago, scientists who were studying the panther noticed that some of the cats had heart problems. Also, mother panthers were giving birth to very few cubs. Along with these problems, many panthers were being killed when they crossed the highways at night. The panther was never very common in the Everglades, but their numbers were dropping fast. Something had to be done.

The panthers were having health problems because they were mating with their sisters, brothers, and cousins. The cats had no choice because there were so few panthers left. Scientists decided to bring some new cats from Texas and let them go free in Florida. This happened about ten years ago and the experiment has been a success. Today, Florida panthers are healthier than they were before, and their numbers are increasing. Now, there are nearly 100 panthers living in southern Florida.

To further protect the panthers, scientists suggested that tall fences be built along the edge of dangerous highways. The fences lead to tunnels that cross beneath the roads so that panthers can safely get from one side of the highway to the other.

All over the world, humans often cause animals to disappear. It's a happy day when people save an animal and allow it to roam free again.

The spots on a baby panther disappear by the time the young cat is one year old.

Wildlife lives in a different world than we do. It is a world we are only beginning to understand. I feel very lucky to have visited the Everglades so many times to watch the wildlife that lives there. I remember laughing when a great blue heron stabbed a large sunfish with its beak and then couldn't get it off to swallow it. Another time, I watched a beautiful golden rat snake hunting in the morning sunshine. Then there was the night I saw a mother opossum with four tiny babies riding on her back like cowboys at a rodeo. Most of all I will never forget the week I spent at a gator hole watching the egrets, storks, and alligators. It was better than any show on television. I hope that someday you also have a chance to explore the Everglades with its sawgrass marshes, gator holes, and tree islands, and take home your own memories of this magnificent wetland ecosystem.

EVERGLADES
WEB SITES

If you want to learn more about the Everglades and the wildlife that lives there, you can search the Internet for the web sites I have listed below. This is where you can learn about the problems facing the Everglades, what people are doing to save it, and how you can help.

Big Cypress National Preserve
www.nps.gov/bicy/

Everglades National Park
www.nps.gov/ever/

Florida Panther Wildlife Refuge
www.floridapanther.org/

Friends of the Everglades
www.everglades.org

Loxahatchee National Wildlife Refuge
www.fws.gov/loxahatchee/home/default.asp

National Hurricane Center
www.nhc.noaa.gov/

National Oceanic & Atmospheric Administration (NOAA)
www.noaa.gov/